JEN BREACH

ROURKE'S SCHOOL to HOME CONNECTIONS
BEFORE AND DURING READING ACTIVITIES

Before Reading: *Building Background Knowledge and Vocabulary*

Building background knowledge can help children process new information and build upon what they already know. Before reading a book, it is important to tap into what children already know about the topic. This will help them develop their vocabulary and increase their reading comprehension.

Questions and Activities to Build Background Knowledge:

1. Look at the front cover of the book and read the title. What do you think this book will be about?
2. What do you already know about this topic?
3. Take a book walk and skim the pages. Look at the table of contents, photographs, captions, and bold words. Did these text features give you any information or predictions about what you will read in this book?

Vocabulary: *Vocabulary Is Key to Reading Comprehension*

Use the following directions to prompt a conversation about each word:

- Read the vocabulary words.
- What comes to mind when you see each word?
- What do you think each word means?

Vocabulary Words:

- celebrates
- colonists
- cuisine
- ethnic
- immigrants
- ingredients
- symbolizes
- taboo

During Reading: *Reading for Meaning and Understanding*

To achieve deep comprehension of a book, children are encouraged to use close reading strategies. During reading, it is important to have children stop and make connections. These connections result in deeper analysis and understanding of a book.

Close Reading a Text

During reading, have children stop and talk about the following:

- Any confusing parts
- Any unknown words
- Text-to-text, text-to-self, text-to-world connections
- The main idea in each chapter or heading

Encourage children to use context clues to determine the meaning of any unknown words. These strategies will help children learn to analyze the text more thoroughly as they read.

When you are finished reading this book, turn to the next-to-last page for After-Reading Questions and an Activity.

TABLE OF CONTENTS

Celebrate Good Times 4

What Do You Get When You Cross Sushi with a Burrito? 12

Made in the USA 22

Recipe: How to Cook Spam Musubi 30

Index 31

After-Reading Questions 31

Activity 31

About the Author 32

Not everyone **celebrates** the same things in the same ways. But for many, celebrating a holiday or a special day includes sharing food that tells a story about themselves, their family or community, their beliefs, or their culture.

celebrates (SEL-uh-braytz): to do something special to mark a happy occasion

Cultural food traditions exist all over the world. Chinese New Year is celebrated by sharing a whole steamed fish, which **symbolizes** unity and luck. In Mexico, Bread of the Dead nourishes visiting souls on Día de los Muertos (Day of the Dead). A Turkish wedding stew called *Keşkek* needs the entire community to make it, including musicians.

TURKEY

symbolizes (SIM-buh-lize-ez): to stand for or represent something else

Food can also be an important part of religious traditions. Judaism, Islam, Buddhism, and Hinduism have rules about what foods to eat, how they should be prepared, and which foods are **taboo**. For example, pork is prohibited for those who are Muslim, many Jewish people do not mix dairy and meat (no cheeseburgers!), and a lot of Hindu people are vegetarian. Many religions also have traditions of fasting, or not eating, for a period of time. Observing these laws and traditions is a way that various cultures celebrate their beliefs.

INDIA

THAILAND

ISRAEL

taboo (tuh-BOO): banned or prohibited according to social or religious custom

HAPPY BIRTHDAY TO YOU!

In the United States, Nicaragua, Germany, Peru, and elsewhere, birthdays are celebrated with cake. Other sweet birthday celebrations include a large fruit pie in Russia, pancakes in the Netherlands, and small truffles in Brazil. Birthday celebrations elsewhere include seaweed soup in South Korea, a noodle dish in China, stacked sandwiches called *migas* in Argentina, and a breakfast of mashed yams and hard-boiled eggs in Ghana.

CHINA

NETHERLANDS

SOUTH KOREA

WHAT DO YOU GET WHEN YOU CROSS SUSHI with a BURRITO?

When people move to a new country, as **colonists** or **immigrants**, they often bring their food traditions with them. Sometimes this results in a fusion **cuisine**, which is a blend of cuisines from different cultures. Tex-Mex is a good example. It combines American and Mexican food to create a cuisine that is a bit of both but not entirely either one.

WHAT DO YOU GET WHEN YOU CROSS SUSHI with a BURRITO?

colonists (KAH-luh-nists): people who live in a colony or who help establish a colony

immigrants (IM-i-gruhntz): people who move from one country to another and settle there

cuisine (kwi-ZEEN): a style or manner of cooking or presenting food

Immigrants might keep up food traditions for comfort, identity, or taste. But their recipes often change when they use new, more accessible **ingredients**. Around 250 years ago, Chinese immigrants in the Goan region of India combined traditional Chinese recipes with Indian spices and vegetables to create new dishes. This became Indian-Chinese fusion cuisine.

ingredients (in-GREE-dee-uhntz): items used to make something

France's colonization of Vietnam in 1884 is still seen in Vietnamese food. Banh mi, the national sandwich of Vietnam, was invented around 1950. It combines traditionally Asian ingredients, like pickled vegetables, cilantro, and grilled meats, with French-introduced bread, pâté, and mayonnaise.

Sometimes, fusion foods are fusions of fusions. In Hawaii, Spam musubi is a popular snack or light lunch. It combines a shaped rice ball from Japanese cuisine with Spam, a tinned, spiced, preserved ham. Spam became popular in Hawaii when American troops stationed there in World War II traded their rations with locals. The result is something most definitely Hawaiian.

19

SOUTH KOREA / MEXICO

UNITED STATES / FRANCE

SOUTH KOREA / GERMANY

WHAT DO YOU GET WHEN YOU CROSS SUSHI with a BURRITO?

A BIT OF THIS AND A BIT OF THAT

Fusion foods can also be made in adventurous restaurant kitchens, in food trucks, or by you. Take some bulgogi and serve it on a tortilla and you have Korean tacos! What if you made a burrito with sushi ingredients? You'd have sushiritos! Everyone loves burgers and everyone loves ramen, right? Put your burger on a ramen noodle bun!

General Tso's chicken is a Chinese cuisine dish, right? Wrong! It was actually created in the United States!

Between 1840 and 1926, thousands of Chinese workers immigrated to California. They often lived in cramped, poor neighborhoods. They adapted their Chinese cooking techniques, such as stir frying and using flavorful sauces, to include local ingredients and began opening restaurants.

To attract American eaters, the restaurants invented new recipes using fried foods and sauces that were sweeter and less spicy. General Tso's chicken was a hit! It was Chinese food that you would never find in China. It was American-Chinese food.

NO PASSPORT NEEDED

Many foods that we think of as being **ethnic** are rumored to have roots in America. Some of these may surprise you: fortune cookies, sesame chicken, chop suey, California sushi rolls, English muffins, Cuban sandwiches, French dressing, Italian dressing, Russian dressing, spaghetti and meatballs, nachos, chili, fajitas, queso, and chimichangas.

ethnic (ETH-nik): of or having to do with a group of people sharing the same national origins, language, or culture

HOW TO COOK SPAM MUSUBI

INGREDIENTS

- 2 tablespoons soy sauce
- 2 tablespoons light brown sugar
- ½ teaspoon mirin (optional)
- 1 (12-ounce) can Spam, cut horizontally into 8 slices
- 1-2 teaspoons neutral oil, like canola or vegetable
- 3 sheets roasted sushi nori
- 5-6 cups cooked short-grain white rice

INSTRUCTIONS

1. In a bowl, stir together soy sauce, sugar, and mirin until sugar is completely dissolved. Marinate sliced Spam in the sauce for at least 5 minutes, or up to an hour.
2. In a large skillet, heat oil over medium-high heat. Cook slices of Spam for 5 minutes per side, or until lightly browned.
3. Cut nori sheets in half and lay on a flat work surface.
4. Shape the cooked rice so it is the same size as the Spam slice. Place it on top of the nori, and top with a slice of Spam. Wrap nori around the rice and Spam, sealing edges with a small amount of water.
5. Serve warm, room temperature, or chilled.

INDEX

Banh mi 16
beliefs 4, 8
birthday(s) 10
colonization 16
fusion 12, 14, 18, 21
General Tso's chicken 22, 26
Spam musubi 18, 30
traditions 6, 8, 12, 14

AFTER-READING QUESTIONS

1. Which country colonized Vietnam?
2. Name four foods that sound ethnic but were actually invented in the United States.
3. If you were eating Keşkek in Turkey, what would the occasion be?
4. Was Indian-Chinese food invented by Chinese people in India or Indian people in China?
5. What is a food that is taboo in Hinduism?

ACTIVITY

If you could create a new fusion cuisine, what two cuisines would you choose to combine? What would a few of your signature dishes be? Draw the dishes you invent, write out the recipes, or write a restaurant-style review of your brand-new food.

ABOUT THE AUTHOR

Jen Breach (pronouns: they/them) is queer and nonbinary. Jen grew up in a tiny town in rural Australia with three older brothers, two parents, and one pet duck. Jen's mum made amazing cakes for everyone's birthday, even the duck's. Jen has worked as an archaeologist, a librarian, an editor, a florist, a barista, a bagel-baker, a code-breaker, a ticket-taker, and a trouble-maker. The best job they ever had was as a writer, which they do now in Philadelphia, Pennsylvania.

© 2023 Rourke Educational Media

All rights reserved. No part of this book may be reproduced or utilized in any form or by any means, electronic or mechanical including photocopying, recording, or by any information storage and retrieval system without permission in writing from the publisher.

www.rourkebooks.com

PHOTO CREDITS: Cover:Rawpixel.com/ Shutterstock.com; pages 4-5: Rawpixel.com/ Shutterstock.com; page 7: Koh Sze Kiat/ Getty Images; page 7: xhico/ Shutterstock.com; page 8: Yavuz Sariyildiz/ Shutterstock.com; page 9: Sakcared/ Shutterstock.com; page 9: Inna Reznik/ Shutterstock.com; page 10: Studio Romantic/ Shutterstock.com; page 11: successo images/ Shutterstock.com; page 11: Boontoom Sae-Kor/ Shutterstock.com; page 11: Ingrid Balabanova/ Shutterstock.com; pages 12-13: Elena Eryomenko/ Shutterstock.com; page 13: Everett Collection/ Shutterstock.com; page 14: bennie/ Shutterstock; pages 14-15: alexreynolds/ Shutterstock.com; page 16: AS Food studio/ Shutterstock.com; pages 16-17: marie martin/ Shutterstock.com; page 18: Bain Collection; page 19: Maridav/ Shutterstock.com; page 19: Brent Hofacker/ Shutterstock.com; page 20: Janet Moore/ Shutterstock.com; page 20: SEE D JAN/ Shutterstock.com; page 20: Brent Hofacker/ Shutterstock.com; page 21: Piotr Piatrouski/ Shutterstock.com; page 21: Ong.thanaong/ Shutterstock.com; page 22: shawnwil23/ Shutterstock.com; pages 22-23: DronG/ Shutterstock.com; page 24: hxdyl/ Shutterstock.com; page 25: Everett Collection/ Shutterstock.com; page 26: Indian Food Images/ Shutterstock.com; pages 26-27: Rawpixel.com/ Shutterstock.com; page 28: Suzanne Tucker/ Shutterstock.com; page 28: Olga Miltsova/ Shutterstock.com; page 29: Catherine77/ Shutterstock.com; page 29: Elena Gordeichik/ Shutterstock.com; page 29: stockcreations/ Shutterstock.com; pages 3, 4, 6, 8, 10-11, 12, 14, 16, 18, 20-21, 22, 24, 26, 28-29, 30-31, 32: Nas photo/ Shutterstock.com; pages 1, 4, 7, 9, 10, 13, 15, 21, 28, 30-31, 32: Lana Veshta/ Shutterstock.com; pages 6-7, 9, 19, 24-25: Ales Krivec on Unsplash

Edited by: Catherine Malaski
Cover and interior design by: Max Porter

Library of Congress PCN Data
From Your Table to the World / Jen Breach
(Food Tour)
ISBN 978-1-73165-273-7 (hard cover)(alk. paper)
ISBN 978-1-73165-236-2 (soft cover)
ISBN 978-1-73165-303-1 (e-book)
ISBN 978-1-73165-333-8 (e-pub)
Library of Congress Control Number: 2021952190

Rourke Educational Media
Printed in the United States of America
03-1362413053